A McGRAW-HILL NEW BIOLOGY

Scientific Adviser: Dr. Gwynne Vevers
Curator of the Aquarium and Invertebrates,
The Zoological Society of London

SEALS

OTHER BOOKS IN THIS SERIES

A McGRAW-HILL NEW BIOLOGY

Robert Burton

Seals

Illustrated by Timothy Bramfitt

McGRAW-HILL BOOK COMPANY
New York   St. Louis   San Francisco

Metric Conversion Table

1 centimeter (cm) = 0.39 inch
1 meter (m) = 3.27 feet
1 kilometer (km) = 0.62 mile

1 sq. centimeter = 0.15 sq. inch
1 sq. metre = 10.76 sq. feet
1 hectare = 2.47 acres
1 sq. kilometer = 0.39 sq. mile

1 kilogram (kg) = 2.21 lb. (avoirdupois)
1 tonne = 0.98 (long) ton

Library of Congress Cataloging in Publication Data

Burton, Robert, 1941–
  Seals.
(A McGraw-Hill new biology)
Includes index.
SUMMARY: Discusses the breeding patterns of seals,
sea lions, and walruses and the development of their
young.
   1. Seals (Animals)—Juvenile literature. [1. Seals
(Animals) 2. Animals—Infancy] I. Bramfitt, Timothy.
II. Title.
QL737.P6B912 1979 599'.745 79–13701
ISBN 0-07-009285-0

First distribution in the United States of America
by McGraw-Hill Book Company, 1979
Text © Robert Burton 1978
Illustrations © Timothy Bramfitt 1978
First printed in Great Britain for
The Bodley Head
by William Clowes (Beccles) Ltd., Beccles
First published 1978
Printed in Great Britain
123456789 7832109

Contents

1

Introduction

Seals are mammals that live in the sea. Like other mammals, seals are warm-blooded and their bodies are covered with hair. They breathe air with their lungs and give birth to living young, which they feed on milk from their mammary glands. Most mammals live on land, but seals have adapted to life at sea.

The ancestors of seals were four-legged, carnivorous, land animals like dogs, otters and bears. Over a period of millions of years they moved into the sea and took to eating fish. To help them swim more rapidly and easily, their bodies slowly changed. The seal's torpedo-shaped body is perfectly designed to slip easily through the water. This smooth, streamlined outline is made by the thick layer of fat, called blubber, under the skin, which also helps to keep the seal warm in cold water. The seal's legs have become flippers for swimming; the long bones in the legs have been shortened to reduce the drag in the water, and the feet have become paddles, rather like the webbed feet of a duck. To make the seal's body more streamlined, the external ear flaps, or pinnae, have grown small or nearly disappeared, and the tail is a mere stump.

Unlike other marine mammals, such as whales,

dolphins and sea-cows, which use their tails to propel them through the water and are helpless on land, seals are not totally aquatic. Although they are at home in the sea, seals have kept some links with their former life on land. Their bodies are covered with hair and they have four limbs with which they can move on land. Seals have lungs rather than gills like fish, so they must come to the surface to breathe air. They also have to "haul out" on land to breed because their babies, called pups, cannot swim properly when newborn.

The Harbor Seal is a true seal. It is clumsy on land.

2

Kinds of seals

The scientific name for the seals is Pinnipedia, which means "fin-footed" and refers to the seals' flippers. There are 31 or 32 species of seals in the world, which are divided into three main types: the true seals in the family Phocidae, the sea-lions and fur seals in the family Otariidae and the Walrus in a family of its own, the Odobenidae.

The true seals are sometimes called earless seals or hair seals. They are not really earless—in fact, like all seals they can hear very well—but their pinnae are tiny and hidden in the fur. The true seals swim with powerful side-to-side movements of their hind-flippers, rather as a fish swims by wriggling its tail. The fore-flippers are used for steering and for swimming slowly. The hind-flippers are permanently turned backwards for swimming and cannot be bent forwards for walking, so true seals are clumsy on land. They hump along slowly on their stomachs, sometimes hitching themselves forwards with their fore-flippers. True seals are found in all the world's oceans. They are most common in the Arctic and Antarctic but some kinds live in warm seas or even in freshwater lakes.

The sea-lions and fur seals are sometimes called eared seals because their pinnae are visible flaps of skin. Unlike the true seals, sea-lions and fur seals are quite agile on land. Sea-lions and fur seals have flexible hind-flippers that can be turned forwards and placed flat on the ground for support so that the body is lifted off the ground. In this way they can gallop along on land quite quickly. In the water sea-lions and fur seals swim with their powerful fore-flippers, which beat up and down as if the seal is flying through the water. The hind-flippers are rarely used when the animal is swimming.

True seals—like this elephant seal —move by humping along.

It is not easy to tell sea-lions and fur seals apart. Fur seals get their name from their thick fur which is made up of two kinds of hair. A short, very dense coat of underfur keeps the body warm and is protected by long, thick guard hairs. Sea-lions have broader, blunter snouts than fur seals and their underfur is less dense. Both sea-lions and fur seals live in cool seas but they do not go into the ice-covered Arctic and Antarctic seas.

Sea-lions swim with their fore-flippers.

The Walrus is different from all other seals.

The Walrus looks rather like a large sea-lion, except that its pinnae are very small and that it has two long tusks. Like the sea-lion and fur seal, it can bend its hind-flippers under its body for walking on land. At sea it swims mainly by using its fore-flippers, rather than its hind-flippers. Its skin is practically naked and very wrinkled. Walruses live in the Arctic Ocean.

3

Seals at sea

All seals are expert swimmers and divers. They dive deep and can stay submerged for a long time while they hunt for food. The record for diving is held by the Weddell Seal of the Antarctic at almost 602 meters' depth and seventy minutes' duration. Most dives are not so long; the usual time for a dive is about five to seven minutes. The Harbor Seal can stay down for about fifteen minutes and the Gray Seal for about twenty. Most people can hold their breath only for about one minute.

A seal's body works in a specialized way so that the animal is able to stay under water for a long time. As soon as a seal dives, its heartbeat automatically slows down, as do all its body processes, such as digestion, that are not directly connected with swimming. This helps to save oxygen so that the seal can stay submerged for a longer period of time. Seals have also developed special ways to deal with the changes in the pressure of water, which occur when the seal dives deep. These changes in pressure may prove fatal to human divers, but they do not bother seals.

Because seals spend nearly all their lives in water, they must be able to keep warm, especially when they live in icy polar seas. Their bodies are insulated by thick layers of blubber, sometimes 5 to 7 cm thick. Fur seals have dense underfur, which works like a thermal undervest by trapping a layer of warm air next to the body. When seals are swimming fast, however, they must have a way of losing the heat produced by their exertions or else they will overheat. The flippers, which have no blubber, act as radiators and allow heat to escape. This is also important when seals are lying on the shore in hot sunshine. Sea-lions and fur seals wave their flippers to help them lose heat and they like to lie in puddles to keep cool. Seals moult their hair once a year.

A fur seal waves its flippers to keep cool.

Weddell Seals live in the Antarctic pack ice.

Very little is known about how seals find their way under water and catch their food. When a seal is below the surface its nostrils and ears are closed. It can still hear, especially the low-pitched sounds such as fish and shrimp make, and seals communicate underwater by calling to one another. Seals' eyes are specially adapted to see well underwater. The pupils dilate, like a cat's eyes, to help see in the dark and contract into slits so that the seal is not dazzled in bright sunlight. Sunlight does not penetrate very deep into water, so it is often too dark and murky for seals to see well. The long whiskers are very sensitive to movements and vibrations underwater. They may help seals to feel their way and to grub for shellfish in the mud. Blind seals can hunt and find their way about perfectly well, which suggests that seals do not depend solely on sight underwater.

All seals are carnivores. They eat fish, squid, crustaceans and shellfish, such as clams, and a few of the larger seals will eat other animals such as penguins. Seals do not have to drink because they get enough water from their food and from sea water, which is swallowed with the food. The sea water does not harm them.

Seals are completely comfortable at sea. They can sleep in the water and be away from land for long periods of time. A seal sleeps at sea in two ways: either it floats vertically at the surface, rather like a floating bottle, with its nose sticking above the surface or it sinks below the surface, and without waking, rises to the surface for air and sinks down again.

Gray Seal "bottling."

4

The breeding season

Some species of seals, especially sea-lions, fur seals and elephant seals, breed in huge colonies. The males, or bulls, which are much bigger than the females, or cows, divide the beach into territories. The aim of each bull is to mark out a territory which he defends by fighting other bulls. He tries to gather as many cows as possible into a "harem" in the territory. The biggest bulls usually get the largest territories and harems, while younger bulls may not even find a cow to mate with.

The pups have to be born out of the water because they cannot swim properly at birth, so the female seals come onto land just before giving birth. Mating usually takes place a few weeks to two months after the birth of the pups. By combining the pupping and mating season, seals need only gather and haul out once a year. Seals return to the same breeding ground year after year, usually to the place where they were born. Breeding always takes place at the same time each year; it is the time that gives the newborn pups the best chance of survival. Some seals, such as the Northern Fur Seal, migrate thousands of kilometers to reach their breeding grounds, and they all arrive at about the same time.

Sea-lion bulls defend territories where they have a "harem" of cows.

Other seals, especially true seals that breed on the polar ice, like the Harp Seals of the Arctic, do not crowd together. The bulls, which are about the same size as the cows, find it difficult to defend a territory and keep away other bulls. They do not establish harems and there is little fighting. Any full-grown bull can mate with the cows.

Cow seal with "whitecoat" pup.

Soon after the cow hauls out she gives birth to a single pup. Twins are very rare. The actual birth is rapid, lasting only a few seconds. The newborn pup is weak and helpless. Its mother stays close by to protect it. But she makes no attempt to cuddle her pup or keep it warm, even when it is born on an ice floe. Within an hour or so of birth, the pup finds its mother's teats and sucks her milk, which is ten times richer in fats than cow or human milk.

Seal pups grow very rapidly.

It is very dangerous for a pup to be separated from its mother. If they do become separated, the pup bleats like a lamb to call its mother. She recognizes her pup by its cry and by its smell. The bulls take no notice of the pups and may even trample them to death during their territorial fights.

Puppyhood is very short among true seals. About three or four weeks after birth, the mothers leave their pups and go back to sea. In these few weeks the pups have usually tripled their birth weight. This is a necessary preparation for the hard months ahead. The pups have to swim out to sea on their own, learn how to catch their food and fend for themselves. Many pups die of starvation or are battered to death by storms. Just before they become independent, the pups shed their first long puppy coat and grow a short coat of fur like the adults.

Sea-lions and fur seals suckle their pups for several months. At intervals the cows go to sea and

Ringed Seal and pup on the Arctic ice.

feed, then return to find their pups and continue feeding them. Walruses suckle their young for over one year and the young may stay with their mothers even after they are weaned.

About two or three weeks after giving birth, the cows are ready to mate with the bulls, who have been waiting on the breeding ground. Mating takes place on land or in the water. Sometimes there is no courtship and the bull simply mounts the cow, grabbing her by the scruff of the neck with his teeth. Other seals, such as the Weddell Seal of the Antarctic and the sea-lions, have a short courtship. The two seals swim or walk around each other, calling and lunging, and the cow may take the initiative. The cows mate many times over a period of a few days, sometimes with several bulls.

The actual mating process in seals is similar to other mammals. The bull lies on the back of the cow, grasping the scruff of her neck with his teeth and placing his fore-flippers around her middle. He thrusts his penis into her vagina, depositing his sperm at the entrance of her womb. One of these sperm joins with an egg inside the female's womb and fertilizes it. It is this fertilized egg that develops into a baby seal. The unborn seal grows inside its mother's womb, well protected and nourished through the umbilical cord, a tube leading from a special organ called the placenta. The cow is pregnant with the pup for about eleven months, which means that she will give birth to a new pup at the same time every year.

Elephant seals.

5

Seals of the Arctic

The Arctic seas are the home of five kinds of true seals—the Harp Seal, Ringed Seal, Bearded Seal, Ribbon Seal and Hooded Seal—which live in the cold, ice-choked water. However, sea water never falls below – 1.8° C, while the air temperature can be very much colder. Since it is often warmer in the water, the seals like to lie on the ice floes only in calm, sunny weather.

The most famous Arctic seal is the Harp Seal because people protest every year when thousands of pups are killed by hunters. The Harp Seal gets its name from the dark, harp-shaped patch of fur on its back. There are three large groups of Harp Seals, one in the White Sea northwest of Russia, one north of Jan Mayen Island in the Greenland Sea and the third in the Gulf of St. Lawrence and the east coast of Newfoundland, Canada. Harp Seals are sociable and 30 or 40 will use one breathing hole in the ice. They have to prevent the hole from freezing solid by chewing newly formed ice.

Ribbon Seal.

The pup of the Harbor Seal spends less time out of water than any other kind of seal. It is born on a sand bank or rock at low tide and it must swim when the tide returns a few hours later. Some Harbor Seal pups are even born in the water, but this is very rare. They have a short waterproof coat like the adults', which enables the newborn pups to swim well, but they are not very good at diving. When danger threatens, the mother seal holds her pup under her fore-flipper and dives with it. At other times she lets it ride on her back.

Although Harbor Seals gather to bask at low tide, they have little to do with each other except during the autumn mating season. They become quite playful, barking and snarling, and pairs of seals roll and splash together. The bulls leap clear of the water in spectacular displays of power.

Gray Seals, also called Atlantic Seals, live on both sides of the North Atlantic. Sometimes they are seen in the same place as Harbor Seals but they prefer cliff-bound coasts and rocky islands. It is not always easy to tell at a glance whether a seal is a Harbor Seal or a Gray Seal. The Gray Seal's head is flatter and longer than the dog-like Harbor Seal and the adult bull has an arched nose. Like the Harbor Seal, Gray Seals gather on favorite rocks and their eerie hooting has become known as the "singing of the seals." The hooting is really the cry of an angry seal when another one comes too close.

Among Gray Seals pupping usually takes place in autumn, rather than in spring as in other seals. Gray Seal pups are born with a white coat. Their mothers immediately turn to sniff them so that, thereafter, they can identify by smell their own pups from among the hundreds in the colony. Sometimes the cows stay on land with their pups but where they can easily slip into the water, they prefer to float off shore except when suckling their pups.

Gray Seal suckling her pup.

7

Gray Seal pup.

The pups spend most of their time asleep. Every four or five hours they wake up hungry and call plaintively. Each cow recognizes the voice of her own pup and comes ashore to suckle it, but she first checks its identity by smell. The meal takes only a few minutes and the pup goes back to sleep. With rich meals and little exercise, the pup grows rapidly, from 14 kg at birth to 45 or 50 kg when it is weaned at three weeks of age. Unless the pups become so fat that they can hardly crawl, they have little hope of surviving the winter. They need a good layer of blubber to keep them going while they learn to fend for themselves. After weaning, the pups spend a couple of weeks ashore before setting out to sea in search of food. Gray Seals, born around the British Isles, wander as far as Norway and Iceland during their first year, but they always return to their birth-place when they are ready to breed at about four years of age.

7

Seals of the Antarctic

The frozen wastes of the Southern Ocean, which surround the continent of Antarctica, are as good a home for seals as the Arctic seas around the North Pole. Until recently, few people had visited the Antarctic and little was known about the seals that live there. Many of them live in the middle of the pack-ice, which ships avoid as much as possible, so they were not often seen. The Ross Seal was once thought to be very rare. It lives among the thickest ice floes and only recently have ships been able to force their way into its home. Very little is known about its habits.

Ross Seal of the Antarctic.

The Crabeater Seal is the most numerous of all seals.

The Crabeater Seal is the commonest of Antarctic seals and groups can be seen from passing ships as they bask on ice floes. The Crabeater Seal's teeth bear rows of sharp points, or cusps, which look as if they are designed to crush the hard shells of crabs. Their true function is to strain small animals from the sea. The main food of the Crabeater Seal is krill, tiny shrimp-like animals that live in teeming swarms in the Southern Ocean. The seal takes a mouthful of krill and water, shuts its mouth, then forces the water out through the gaps between the cusps of its teeth. The krill are left inside the mouth

31

and are swallowed. Some Crabeater Seals have rows of huge scars running down their bodies. These were probably made by Leopard Seals, which attack young Crabeaters.

The Leopard Seal, so-called because of its spotted coat, has a reputation for being very fierce. It is larger than the other Antarctic Seals. Its head is huge and its mouth is lined with sharp teeth, so it looks dangerous and it hunts baby seals and penguins. The bad reputation has not been improved by stories of Leopard Seals following small boats and

Leopard Seals hunting penguins.

even chasing people over the ice. The seal is only curious. If you run away, it follows to get a closer look.

The main food of Leopard Seals is krill, fish and squid but some individuals specialize in hunting penguins. They lie in wait in shallow water and chase unwary penguins as they travel to and from their colonies. The penguins are not safe even on the ice because the seals can climb on to ice floes to chase them or smash up through thin ice to get penguins walking over the surface. The penguins know that Leopard Seals are dangerous and try to avoid ambushes. They run across thin ice as fast as possible, avoid cracks where a seal may be lurking and do not loiter in shallow water near the shore. Despite their big mouths and sharp teeth, Leopard Seals are

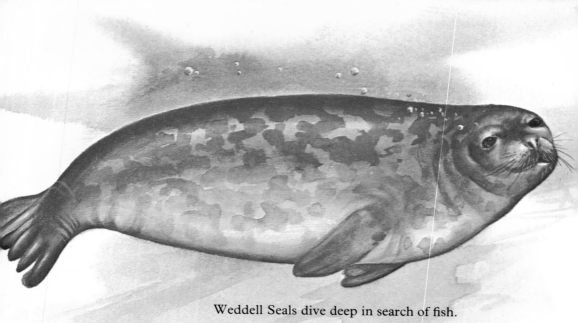

Weddell Seals dive deep in search of fish.

finicky feeders. Although they could easily crunch up a penguin, they prefer to shake it violently so that pieces of meat are torn off, and the skeleton is left undamaged.

The Weddell Seal lives around the coasts of Antarctica. It prefers the solid ice attached to the shore and is not so common in the drifting pack-ice. Its home is under the ice and it surfaces to breathe either at cracks or at holes, which it makes by chewing through the ice with its teeth.

Weddell Seals are deep divers. They regularly hunt for fish at depths of 200 to 400 meters but they have to come out of the water to breed. The cows gather in groups near the cracks or holes at the end of the long Antarctic winter, when the weather is still very cold, and the bulls take up their positions under the ice. They call to each other with strange chugging sounds and high-pitched, bird-like trills. Fights sometimes break out and many bulls are badly gashed and pieces are torn out of their flippers.

The Weddell Seal's birth must be a great shock. It leaves the warmth of its mother's body and flops on to the ice, which is 50° C colder, in a matter of seconds. This is worse than jumping from a hot bath into a freezing pond. At first the pup is weak and shivering but its mother's milk soon gives it strength and it grows rapidly. Weddell Seal pups usually have their first swim when they are two or three weeks old but some have their first dip when only a couple of days old. Although most seal pups take to the water unaccompanied, Weddell Seal pups are escorted by their mothers. The cow may drag her reluctant pup into the water by the scruff of its neck and the pair will swim and play together. After the swim, the pup may have to be helped back onto the ice.

A Weddell Seal coaxes her pup into the water.

8
Elephant seals and monk seals

The two species of elephant seals are the largest of the seals, larger even than Walruses. Adult bulls weigh over 3,500 kg and measure 6 meters from head to tail. The cows are much smaller, only 900 kg and 3.5 meters. The enormous nose of the adult bull, from which the elephant seal gets its name, can be inflated to make a huge cushion that hangs over the mouth. The Northern Elephant Seal lives on islands off the coast of California and Mexico and the Southern Elephant Seal lives on subantarctic islands such as South Georgia and the Falkland Islands.

Elephant seals have spectacular fights
in the breeding season.

For all their great bulk, elephant seals are fine swimmers. The southern species feeds on fast-moving squid and the northern seals eat sharks and other fish. Movement is more difficult on land yet the bulls travel at a surprising speed. They bounce down the beach like gigantic brown jellies but, after only a few meters, they have to flop down and rest. Elephant seals are usually lazy on land and they have to be very upset before they retreat into the sea. The breeding season brings a burst of activity. The cows gather in harems and the largest bulls, called beach-masters, attempt to drive away rivals, and fights break out. They rear up, facing each other with

noses inflated, crashing their bodies together and slashing one another with their teeth. Meanwhile the cows are giving birth and suckling black, woolly-coated pups. The pups do not enter the water for the first five weeks and they become independent at about ten weeks.

A few months after the breeding season, the elephant seals return to the beaches to moult. This process can be catastrophic for elephant seals. Large sheets of skin fall off so that the seal looks quite revolting. The moulting seals gather in muddy pools to soothe the irritation caused by the moult. They cram together, one on top of another, and lie there for days. Sometimes the ones at the bottom of the pile drown because they cannot get out.

Elephant seals gather on beaches when they moult.

Monk seals are the only true seals living in warm seas.

The monk seals are the only true seals living in warm water. Of the three species, the West Indian is probably extinct from hunting but the Hawaiian is reasonably abundant. The Mediterranean Monk Seal now numbers only about 500 animals, which are scattered around the Mediterranean, the Black Sea and the northwest coast of Africa. In the times of the ancient Greeks and Romans, the Mediterranean Monk Seal was very common and its skin was used for making tents.

9

Sea-lions and fur seals

The Californian Sea-lion is the "performing seal" of circus and zoo. It is the smallest of the sea-lions and the bull lacks the shaggy mane that gives the sea-lions their name. Many seals are naturally playful and inquisitive, and Californian Sea-lions sometimes pick stones from the sea bed, toss them into the air and catch them. As sea-lions are intelligent as well as inquisitive, they are an obvious choice of animal to be taught tricks. Trained sea-lions are also used to recover objects lost on the sea bed. The sea-lion dives with a special clamp on the end of a rope. It attaches the clamp to the object and it is then pulled to the surface. Trained sea-lions also carry messages and tools to divers.

Sea-lions learn tricks
with ease.

Steller's Sea-lion.

Sea-lions live all the year round on beaches and small islands mostly in the Pacific Ocean. They are usually quite tame but, during the breeding season, the bulls defend their territories against all comers, including human beings. A one ton Steller's Sea-lion charging down the beach is a frightening sight. The cows also defend their pups from any seal or person who comes too close. The Californian Sea-lion suckles her pup up to one year, much longer than other species of seals.

The Northern Fur Seal is the only fur seal to live in the northern hemisphere, except for the rare Guadalupe Fur Seal, which lives on the island of Guadalupe off Lower California. The other fur seals live in the southern oceans and sometimes use the same beaches as sea-lions, but the two keep apart. A surprising discovery was made a few years ago when American scientists found a small group of Northern Fur Seals breeding among sea-lions on the coast of California. Their usual home is Alaska, thousands of kilometers to the north.

Some species of fur seal nearly became extinct.

A newborn fur seal has a dark coat.

In the past, millions of fur seals were slaughtered for their fine fur. A long and delicate treatment is needed to remove the long guard hairs from the pelt and expose the rich, soft underfur but the furs were so valuable that fur seals were hunted nonetheless.

Some species of fur seal were almost exterminated by the hunters but they are now regaining their numbers through careful conservation. Once again the beaches swarm every summer as thousands of fur seal cows come ashore to bear their pups. The pups are suckled for three months and, while their mothers are away fishing, they gather in gangs to play. They romp in the sea and chase birds until they become hungry. Then each pup goes back to the spot where it left its mother and waits for her return. The mother lands where she left her pup and walks up the beach, calling at intervals. On hearing her, the pup calls back and they both thread their way through the throngs of seals until they are reunited.

10

Walrus

The Walrus is quite unlike other seals, although it looks rather like a huge sea-lion. A large male Walrus weighs 1,300 kg and measures 3.6 meters from nose to tail. The Walrus has thick, wrinkled skin covered with short, sparse hairs and is the only seal to have a pair of long ivory tusks, which both the males and females have when they are full-grown. These tusks may grow more than a meter long. One way that the Walrus uses its tusks is as a lever for pulling itself out of the water and onto the ice. Another unique feature is the pair of throat

Walrus and pup.

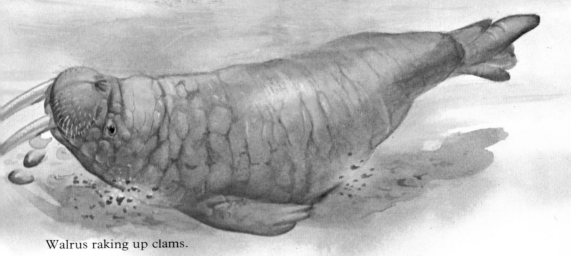
Walrus raking up clams.

pouches which are inflated with air like a life jacket to keep the Walrus afloat while it sleeps in the water.

Walruses live around the Arctic Ocean and are most common along the edge of the pack-ice. Sometimes hundreds gather in groups, which are called *uglit* by the Eskimos. A few Walruses stray southwards and, on very rare occasions, they visit British coasts. They prefer shallow water where they can dive to the bottom for food. Their favorite food is cockles and clams, although they also eat some fish, crabs and sea worms. Cockles and clams live in the mud and gravel of the sea bed and the Walruses stir them up with their tusks. They are gathered with the whiskers but no one knows how the Walrus actually eats them. Somehow it manages to extract the animal from the shell, perhaps by sucking. Two thousand clams can be eaten in a single meal, yet not a single shell is swallowed. Some Walruses make a habit of eating the pups of Ringed and Bearded Seals, or even young Walruses.

45

Unlike most other seals, Walruses do not give birth every year. Their pups grow up extremely slowly and they live on their mothers' milk for over a year. They continue to be suckled during their second year while they learn to find their own food. Even then, they may stay with their mothers because their tusks have not grown long enough to stir up clams properly and they need help from adult Walruses.

The Walrus pup, weighing 45 kg, is born on an ice floe. Although it can swim when it is a few days old, the pup prefers to keep dry. It does not have as much fur and blubber as other seal pups to keep it warm. For the first two or three months of its life, its mother cuddles it to keep it warm, unlike any other seal. When she wants to swim to another ice floe, she sometimes carries the pup on her back.

Walruses can be very fierce, especially when they are defending their pups. Polar Bears and Killer Whales eat pups and half-grown Walruses but they are attacked and even killed by adults. The only other enemy the Walrus has is man, who has ruthlessly hunted the Walrus for its fine ivory tusks.

Walrus pups greeting each other.

Index